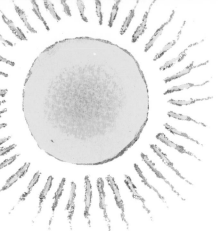

Modeh Ani

A Good Morning Book

בֹּקֶר טוֹב

מוֹדֶה אֲנִי

Adapted by Sarah Gershman
Illustrated by Kristina Swarner

EKS PUBLISHING
Oakland, Californ

In loving memory of Beth Samuels

Modeh Ani: A Good Morning Book

Copyright © 2010 by Sarah Gershman

Printed in The United States

EKS Publishing Co.
PO Box 9750
Berkeley, CA 94709-0750
email: orders@ekspublishing.com
Phone: (510) 251-9100
Fax: (510) 251-9102

ISBN 978-0-939144-63-1 (paperback)
ISBN 978-0-939144-64-8 (hardcover)
First Printing, April 2010

Library of Congress Cataloging-in-Publication Data:

Gershman, Sarah, 1972-
Modeh ani : a good morning book / adapted by Sarah Gershman ;
Illustrated by Kristina Swarner.
p. cm.
Includes the text of selections from the Morning benedictions
in Hebrew with English translation.
ISBN 978-0-939144-63-1 (pbk.) — ISBN 978-0-939144-64-8 (hardcover)
1. Morning benedictions—Adaptations—Juvenile literature.
2. Judaism—Prayers and devotions. I. Swarner, Kristina.
II. Morning benedictions. English & Hebrew. Selections. III. Title.
BM670.M67G47 2010
296.4'5—dc22
2010011759

Thank you God for

waking me from my sleep.

You help me distinguish

between day and night.

שמע ישראל יי אלהינו יי אחד

Listen Israel. God is our God. God is One.

Sh'ma Yisrael Adonai Eloheinu Adonai Echad

How wonderful is God's world.

Baruch shem k'vod malchuto l'olam va' ed

ברוך שם כבוד מלכותו לעולם ועד

You give me eyes that open.

May I see the goodness in people.

Each part of me fits together like a puzzle.
Thank you God for my body.

You created me in your image

and there is no one else quite like me.

Thank you God for my soul.

I am blessed with a home.

May it be filled with joy.

I am blessed with people that love me.

May I give love to others and help those in need.

I am excited to explore and ask questions.
Thank you God that I am able to learn.

May I soar to new heights

under the shelter of your wings.

Thank you God
for this new day.

בִּרְכוֹת הַשַּׁחַר

Excerpts from the Morning Blessings

מוֹדֶה/מוֹדָה אֲנִי לְפָנֶיךָ, מֶלֶךְ חַי וְקַיָּם, שֶׁהֶחֱזַרְתָּ בִּי נִשְׁמָתִי בְּחֶמְלָה; רַבָּה אֱמוּנָתֶךָ.

I give thanks before you, God, living and eternal Ruler, for returning my soul to me with
compassion. How great is your faith in me!

מַה יָּקָר חַסְדְּךָ, אֱלֹהִים, וּבְנֵי אָדָם בְּצֵל כְּנָפֶיךָ יֶחֱסָיוּן. יִרְוְיֻן מִדֶּשֶׁן בֵּיתֶךָ, וְנַחַל עֲדָנֶיךָ
תַשְׁקֵם. כִּי עִמְּךָ מְקוֹר חַיִּים, בְּאוֹרְךָ נִרְאֶה אוֹר. מְשֹׁךְ חַסְדְּךָ לְיֹדְעֶיךָ, וְצִדְקָתְךָ לְיִשְׁרֵי לֵב.

How precious is your kindness, God! Your children are protected in the shadow of your wings. May
they be nourished from the plenty of your house, and may you give them to drink from the river of
your delights. For with you is the source of life. Through your light we see light. Show your kindness
to those who know you and your righteousness to the straight of heart.

מַה טֹּבוּ אֹהָלֶיךָ יַעֲקֹב, מִשְׁכְּנֹתֶיךָ יִשְׂרָאֵל. וַאֲנִי בְּרֹב חַסְדְּךָ אָבוֹא בֵיתֶךָ, אֶשְׁתַּחֲוֶה אֶל הֵיכַל
קָדְשְׁךָ בְּיִרְאָתֶךָ. יי אָהַבְתִּי מְעוֹן בֵּיתֶךָ, וּמְקוֹם מִשְׁכַּן כְּבוֹדֶךָ. וַאֲנִי אֶשְׁתַּחֲוֶה וְאֶכְרָעָה,
אֶבְרְכָה לִפְנֵי יי עֹשִׂי. וַאֲנִי, תְפִלָּתִי לְךָ יי, עֵת רָצוֹן, אֱלֹהִים בְּרָב חַסְדֶּךָ, עֲנֵנִי בֶּאֱמֶת יִשְׁעֶךָ.

How goodly are your tents, Jacob, your dwellings, Israel. Through your kindness I will come into
your house. In awe of you, I will bow down towards your holy Sanctuary. God, I love the house
where you reside and the place where your glory dwells. I will bow down before you God, my
Maker. May my prayers to you, God, come at the right time. God, with your great kindness,
answer me with the truth of your salvation.

בָּרוּךְ אַתָּה יי אֱלֹהֵינוּ מֶלֶךְ הָעוֹלָם, אֲשֶׁר יָצַר אֶת הָאָדָם בְּחָכְמָה, וּבָרָא בוֹ נְקָבִים נְקָבִים,
חֲלוּלִים חֲלוּלִים. גָּלוּי וְיָדוּעַ לִפְנֵי כִסֵּא כְבוֹדֶךָ, שֶׁאִם יִפָּתֵחַ אֶחָד מֵהֶם, אוֹ יִסָּתֵם אֶחָד
מֵהֶם, אִי אֶפְשָׁר לְהִתְקַיֵּם וְלַעֲמוֹד לְפָנֶיךָ. בָּרוּךְ אַתָּה יי, רוֹפֵא כָל בָּשָׂר וּמַפְלִיא לַעֲשׂוֹת.

Blessed are you God, our God, Ruler of the Universe, who made the human being with wisdom,
and created in us many openings and many holes. It is clear before your throne of Glory that if one
of them were to rupture or be blocked, we could not live and stand before you. Blessed are you God,
who heals all flesh and makes wonders.

בָּרוּךְ אַתָּה יי אֱלֹהֵינוּ מֶלֶךְ הָעוֹלָם, אֲשֶׁר קִדְּשָׁנוּ בְּמִצְוֹתָיו, וְצִוָּנוּ לַעֲסוֹק בְּדִבְרֵי תוֹרָה.

Blessed are you God, our God, Ruler of the Universe, who makes us holy through God's commandments, and commands us to engage in the words of Torah.

וְהַעֲרֶב נָא יי אֱלֹהֵינוּ אֶת דִּבְרֵי תוֹרָתְךָ בְּפִינוּ וּבְפִי עַמְּךָ בֵּית יִשְׂרָאֵל, וְנִהְיֶה אֲנַחְנוּ וְצֶאֱצָאֵינוּ וְצֶאֱצָאֵי עַמְּךָ בֵּית יִשְׂרָאֵל, כֻּלָּנוּ יוֹדְעֵי שְׁמֶךָ וְלוֹמְדֵי תוֹרָתֶךָ לִשְׁמָהּ. בָּרוּךְ אַתָּה יי, הַמְלַמֵּד תּוֹרָה לְעַמּוֹ יִשְׂרָאֵל.

God, please sweeten the words of your Torah in our mouths and in the mouth of your people, the House of Israel. May we and our children and the children of your people, the House of Israel, know your name and study your Torah for its own sake. Blessed are you God, teacher of Torah to God's people, Israel.

אֱלֹהַי, נְשָׁמָה שֶׁנָּתַתָּ בִּי טְהוֹרָה הִיא. אַתָּה בְרָאתָהּ, אַתָּה יְצַרְתָּהּ, אַתָּה נְפַחְתָּהּ בִּי, וְאַתָּה מְשַׁמְּרָהּ בְּקִרְבִּי, וְאַתָּה עָתִיד לִטְּלָהּ מִמֶּנִּי, וּלְהַחֲזִירָהּ בִּי לֶעָתִיד לָבֹא. כָּל זְמַן שֶׁהַנְּשָׁמָה בְקִרְבִּי, מוֹדֶה אֲנִי לְפָנֶיךָ, יי אֱלֹהַי וֵאלֹהֵי אֲבוֹתַי, רִבּוֹן כָּל הַמַּעֲשִׂים, אֲדוֹן כָּל הַנְּשָׁמוֹת. בָּרוּךְ אַתָּה יי, הַמַּחֲזִיר נְשָׁמוֹת לִפְגָרִים מֵתִים.

My God, the soul you have given me is pure. You created it, you formed it, and you breathed it into me; and you guard it within me, and in the future will take it away from me, and return it to me in the time to come. As long as my soul is within me, I am grateful to you, God, my God, the God of my ancestors, Master of all creation, Ruler of all souls. Blessed are you God, who restores our souls.

בָּרוּךְ אַתָּה יי אֱלֹהֵינוּ מֶלֶךְ הָעוֹלָם, אֲשֶׁר נָתַן לַשֶּׂכְוִי בִינָה לְהַבְחִין בֵּין יוֹם וּבֵין לַיְלָה.

Blessed are you God, our God, Ruler of the Universe, who gave us wisdom to distinguish between day and night.

בָּרוּךְ אַתָּה יי אֱלֹהֵינוּ מֶלֶךְ הָעוֹלָם, הַמַּעֲבִיר שֵׁנָה מֵעֵינַי וּתְנוּמָה מֵעַפְעַפָּי.

Blessed are you God, our God, Ruler of the Universe, who removes sleep from my eyes and heaviness from my eyelids.

וִיהִי רָצוֹן מִלְּפָנֶיךָ, יי אֱלֹהֵינוּ וֵאלֹהֵי אֲבוֹתֵינוּ, שֶׁתַּרְגִּילֵנוּ בְּתוֹרָתֶךָ, וְדַבְּקֵנוּ בְּמִצְוֹתֶיךָ, וְאַל תְּבִיאֵנוּ לֹא לִידֵי חֵטְא, וְלֹא לִידֵי עֲבֵרָה וְעָוֹן, וְלֹא לִידֵי נִסָּיוֹן, וְלֹא לִידֵי בִזָּיוֹן, וְאַל תַּשְׁלֵט בָּנוּ יֵצֶר הָרָע. וְהַרְחִיקֵנוּ מֵאָדָם רָע וּמֵחָבֵר רָע. וְדַבְּקֵנוּ בְּיֵצֶר הַטּוֹב וּבְמַעֲשִׂים טוֹבִים, וְכוֹף אֶת יִצְרֵנוּ לְהִשְׁתַּעְבֶּד לָךְ. וּתְנֵנוּ הַיּוֹם, וּבְכָל יוֹם, לְחֵן, לְחֶסֶד וּלְרַחֲמִים בְּעֵינֶיךָ, וּבְעֵינֵי כָל רוֹאֵינוּ, וְתִגְמְלֵנוּ חֲסָדִים טוֹבִים. בָּרוּךְ אַתָּה יי, גּוֹמֵל חֲסָדִים טוֹבִים לְעַמּוֹ יִשְׂרָאֵל.

May it be Your will God, our God, and God of our ancestors, that we walk in the ways of your Torah and cling to your commandments. Do not bring us to do the wrong thing. Let not our evil inclination control us. Distance us from bad people and bad friends. Help us cling to our good inclination and to good deeds, and help our will to serve you. Give us today and each day grace, kindness, mercy in your eyes and in the eyes of all who see us, and give us absolute kindness. Blessed are you God, who bestows absolute kindness to God's people, Israel.

שְׁמַע יִשְׂרָאֵל, יי אֱלֹהֵינוּ, יי אֶחָד.

Listen Israel. God is our God. God is One.

בָּרוּךְ שֵׁם כְּבוֹד מַלְכוּתוֹ לְעוֹלָם וָעֶד.

Blessed is the Name of God's glorious Kingdom forever and ever.

וְאָהַבְתָּ אֵת יי אֱלֹהֶיךָ, בְּכָל לְבָבְךָ, וּבְכָל נַפְשְׁךָ, וּבְכָל מְאֹדֶךָ. וְהָיוּ הַדְּבָרִים הָאֵלֶּה, אֲשֶׁר אָנֹכִי מְצַוְּךָ הַיּוֹם, עַל לְבָבֶךָ. וְשִׁנַּנְתָּם לְבָנֶיךָ, וְדִבַּרְתָּ בָּם, בְּשִׁבְתְּךָ בְּבֵיתֶךָ, וּבְלֶכְתְּךָ בַדֶּרֶךְ, וּבְשָׁכְבְּךָ, וּבְקוּמֶךָ. וּקְשַׁרְתָּם לְאוֹת עַל יָדֶךָ, וְהָיוּ לְטֹטָפֹת בֵּין עֵינֶיךָ. וּכְתַבְתָּם עַל מְזֻזוֹת בֵּיתֶךָ וּבִשְׁעָרֶיךָ.

And you shall love God, Your God, with all your heart, with all your body, and with everything that you have. May you take to heart these things that I command you today. Teach them to your children. Speak of them when you sit in your home, when you walk on the way, when you lie down and when you rise up. Put them as a sign on your arm and *tefillin* between your eyes. Write them on the doorposts of your house and on your gates.

About *Modeh Ani*

Weekday mornings in our home, as in many homes, are hurried affairs. We rush through the list of daily tasks—rarely taking a moment to stop and appreciate the arrival of a new day. Amidst the flurry of dressing, preparing breakfast and packing lunches, there is hardly time for reading a book to our children. Yet, it is precisely at this time of day that our family most needs a book like this one. My hope is that *Modeh Ani* will provide families with a calming and focusing ritual—a way to celebrate God's daily gifts to us and prepare us for the day to come.

Modeh Ani is based on selections from *Birchot HaShachar*, the Morning Blessings that are part of *Shacharit*, the daily morning prayer service. The power of these prayers comes from the juxtaposition of the mundane and the profound, the human and the divine. We give thanks for blessings both small and large, such as the ability to open our eyes and the rising of the sun—both powerful displays of God's splendor.

We begin our day by saying the *Modeh Ani* prayer, which expresses our gratitude for our very lives. In the prayers that follow, we thank God for many gifts: for the workings of our bodies, whether they be intellectual or physical abilities, and for being created in God's image.

The *Shulchan Aruch*, the famous code of Jewish law, tells us that a person "should get up early enough to welcome in the dawn" (Chapter 1). Many parents know all too well the challenges of early risers. And yet this idea of welcoming the sun each day is profound. This simple (albeit difficult) act offers us an opportunity to witness the daily miracle of sunrise—and thus begin the day with holiness, joy, and peace.

Boker Tov, Good Morning!

Sarah Gershman